JOURNEY *to* CHRISTMAS

A Yuletide Story for Children of All Ages

WAYNE SKINNER

Illustrated by Bruce Gebert

PAULIST PRESS   NEW YORK / MAHWAH, N.J.

To Annie and Sarah

Copyright 1996 by Wayne Skinner

Library of Congress Cataloging-in-Publication Data

Skinner, Wayne.

Journey to Christmas : a yuletide story for children of all ages / by Wayne Skinner : illustrated by Bruce Gebert.

p.   cm.

Summary: A visit to their grandparents' farm allows Emma, Barney, and Will to experience a country Christmas and realize the deep meaning of the birth of Christ.

ISBN 0-8091-6634-8 (alk. paper)

[1. Christmas—Fiction.   2. Christian life—Fiction. 3. Country life—Fiction.   4. Grandparents—Fiction.] I. Gebert, Bruce, ill.   II. Title.

PZ7.S62815Jo   1996

[Fic]—dc20   96-12503

CIP

AC

Published by Paulist Press
997 Macarthur Boulevard, Mahwah, New Jersey 07430

Design and Composition: Wilsted & Taylor Publishing Services

Printed and bound in the United States of America

WHEN I was young, we used to spend Christmas with my grandparents. They lived on a big, old farm in the country. There was always snow then—lots of it.

We had to get there by train. Mom and Dad had a special savings account where they put aside some money every month to make sure we could afford to make the journey to see Grandpa and Grandma.

We usually left the day before Christmas Eve. First, we had to pile everything into our old car for the drive to the train station. We would have lots of packages and things to bring with us. The car was crammed full.

You could count on my brothers, Barney and Will, to fight during the ride to the station. My sister, Em, sat up front with Mom and Dad, being ever so good until Will pulled one of her pigtails.

"Stop it, boys—you need to be good for Christmas!" Mom said, pleadingly.

"This is going to be a long trip . . ." Dad sighed as we pulled into the train station.

The one thing I remember about the train ride was that it always started with great excitement. We could hardly stay in our seats, although Mom tried her best to get us to stay put. And the conductor, who at other times was stern with kids, was less irritated than usual by our running around the train car. He even gave out candy canes to the children.

Dad slept, or looked out the window at the trees and fields, so full of new winter snow. By the end of the train ride, which took forever—forever being defined back then

as about half a day—we were all napping upon our arrival at the train station, except for Mom who woke us, saying, "Come on, sleepyheads, or we'll end up in Timbuktu."

We tumbled out of the train into a land of snow. Not only was the snow already knee-deep, but it still was falling heavily. We all hurried inside to look for Grandpa, except for Dad, who had to get our luggage.

"How are we gonna get to the farm?" Bar-

ney asked Grandpa, who—after he'd given each of us a big hug—stood back and gave us all a long, admiring look.

"We'll never make it by car," Grandpa said. "We never would have got here to meet you either. It's been snowing steadily since bedtime last night."

"Well, how did you get here?" asked Em, with a puzzled look on her face.

"Come and see," said Grandpa, as he put on his thick fur hat and headed for the door. We walked out to what used to be the street but now was a world that had turned all white.

"Over here," he said, going around the corner of the station. There were two of his strongest work horses, tied up to a great big sleigh.

"You fixed it up," said Dad, patting Grandpa on the back. "It looks great!"

"Well, thanks," Grandpa replied. "We had a lot of rainy days this fall, with not much else

to do. Working on this old beauty of a sleigh kept me from going stir crazy."

"That sleigh belonged to Grandpa's father—your great-grandfather!" Dad said. "I remember how much we used to rely on it every winter."

"Wow! Come on!" shouted Barney. "Let's go to the farm!"

We all climbed in, getting under the heavy blankets that Grandpa had brought along to make sure we stayed warm on the ride to the farm.

"On, Dasher! On, Prancer!" Grandpa called to the horses as we headed out.

"That's not their names, Grandpa—is it?" Em asked, not quite sure of herself. "Those are Santa's reindeer."

"No, I was just kidding," Grandpa admitted. "But on the day before Christmas Eve, I just got to thinking."

"Actually, their real names are Comet and Blitzen," Barney piped in.

"Are not," Em insisted.

"Are too," Barney countered.

As the light began to fade from the sky, Em and Barney continued teasing one another, with Will joining in. Grandpa told us that the horses were really called Boxer and Bonnie. That was good enough to turn Em and Barney and Will's attention away from their argument to the matter of who would hold the reins. "Not tonight," Grandpa said. "Another time—when the weather's better and the roads are safer."

We were all quiet and warm as Boxer and Bonnie made their way over snow-clogged roads that would see no cars or trucks until the next day when the snow plow came through. But that snowy evening, Grandpa's horses and sleigh carried us safely and magically to the farm. We did not know it then, but we were on our real journey to Christmas.

THE next day was Christmas Eve. By the time we awoke, Grandpa and Dad had done just about all the chores, including feeding the animals and milking Elsie, the one cow that Grandpa still had. Bringing in the milk as we sat at the table having porridge and Grandma's fresh-made bread, Dad said, "Good morning, sleepyheads! Come and give us a hand making a path to the road." We rushed to grab our coats and boots. "Don't forget your caps and mittens," Grandma called after us.

It was cold, but the sun was so bright that we squinted and tears came to our eyes. Shoveling the snow, we didn't have to worry about being too cold. After we finished shoveling, we tried to make snowmen but the snow wasn't sticky enough.

We stayed outside playing, coming in only for lunch—Grandma's bread with molasses on it, or some cheese, and a glass of fresh milk. As we gobbled down our food and hurried to get dressed again, the smells from the kitchen promised us ham for dinner and Mom's lemon meringue pie for dessert. We rushed out to spend the afternoon in play, knowing that, hungry and tired as we would be by evening, there would be something special waiting to fill our bellies and revive our spirits. Grandma would not have to worry about whether we would come running when she asked Mom to ring the dinner bell and call us to the table.

That was the afternoon that Will's snow house collapsed on him. The path that we had all helped Grandpa and Dad shovel to the road had produced big banks on either side. When we went out after lunch, Barney yelled, "I'm gonna build a snow cave of my own in the snow bank, and I don't want any help!"

"Well, I'm gonna build one of my own, too, way better than yours," Em shouted back.

"Just wait till you see mine," Will challenged everyone.

Pretty soon we were all building our own caves. Em and Will, seeing that the steepest banks near the house were taken, noticed that there were even better ones near the road. They ran out and claimed their spots. Will found the best spot of all right by the side of the road. He set to work to build the biggest and best snow cave on the entire planet Earth.

The snow plow had been by early in the morning, clearing just enough of a path to allow two cars to barely pass, if they were very careful. The plow had dumped a big pile of snow in front of the driveway. Dad insisted on shoveling it himself, so that Grandpa

wouldn't have to do it. Will's spot was the big hill of snow that Dad had made.

When the snow plow came around the bend for the second time, nobody expected it. Will was busy inside his cave, digging deeper into the snow bank.

Em was the one who saw it coming. She was just stepping back to see how her efforts to build the perfect snow cave compared with

the others. The rest of us were totally caught up in our cave-building.

Em saw the snow plow pushing back the snow it had piled up earlier. She turned to see where Will was. When she didn't see him, she called to him, but there was no answer, so she started to run. The plow continued forward, cutting into the hill where Will was building the best snow cave ever. As the whole hill moved, Em saw Will's arm reach

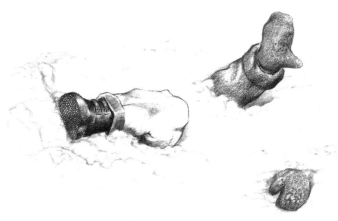

out, and then the snow closed in around it as the plow moved on down the road.

When she reached the spot where Will's cave had been, Em saw no sign of Will. She screamed back toward the house and frantically dug at the snow with her hands. She dug low in the bank, where she had seen his arm go under. She called, "Will! Will!" And then she saw his parka. Scratching away the snow, she quickly got to his face. Poor Will wasn't moving at all. His eyes were closed, and snow filled his nose and mouth.

When the rest of us finally reached Will, Em was clearing the snow from his mouth. Will wasn't breathing and except for his face

and arm, he remained stuck in the snow pile. We quickly started digging to get Will's body free.

As we did, we could hear Grandpa and Dad and Mom running up to the road to see what was the matter. By the time they got there, we had gotten most of the snow off Will, but he still wasn't moving. Dad lifted him out of the bank and carefully laid him face-down on the path. He pushed on Will's back while Grandpa moved Will's arms up and down. We all watched, too shocked to say a word.

Then, all of a sudden, Will let out a great gasp and started breathing in panicky gulps. Dad turned him on his back and pumped his legs to help him get his breath. Will looked dazed and confused as he stared up at all of us watching him. As Mom bent down to hold him, he started to cry. Maybe it was the bright sun, but the rest of us had watery eyes too.

WE didn't do much the rest of the afternoon. We mostly sat inside, looking
out, or over by Will, who was so exhausted
that he lay sleeping on the sofa in Grandma's
living room. Everyone said that Em had saved
Will's life, that if she hadn't noticed what the
snow plow had done, that if she hadn't rushed
to find him, that if she hadn't called for help
. . . well, "we wouldn't be thinking at all
about Christmas"—that was how Grandma
had put it.

Mom and Dad were really shaken up
about it. And Em, poor Em, she was confused, what with everyone calling her a hero.
It wasn't as if she had been trying to save

Will's life, or had even thought about what was happening—it was just that everything had happened so fast that she was just trying to make sure Will was safe. She didn't know what to make of what had happened.

Will had just been glad to have Mom hugging him. Dad lifted him back to the house and carefully checked to make sure Will didn't have any cuts or broken bones.

"You're gonna come out of this with nothing more than a few bruises and a wrecked snow cave, my boy," was what he said when he realized that Will was going to be okay. "This is one tough snow miner we have here, Maggie," he said to Mom. "He could probably use a cup of hot cocoa," Dad suggested.

"Come to think of it, I bet everyone could," Mom said, knowing that was our favorite winter treat.

We sat around and looked out the window. We knew that our cousins would be arriving by nightfall. Uncle Ned and Aunt Marie had a son, Tim, and a daughter, Nell. Aunt Freda and Uncle Jim had a daughter, Kathleen. They were driving up together. They arrived just as it was getting dark. We hurried out to greet them, each of us joining in to tell them the story of our ride on Grandpa's sleigh and the snow caves and how the plow had buried Will and how Em had saved his life.

Even Will began to stir when everyone came into the house. He was the center of everyone's attention, and he liked it. Em was beginning to believe that maybe she was a hero after all. All the adults appeared amazed by the details of the story, and they couldn't stop talking about it.

Dinner was served soon after everyone got settled. All the smells of the day's cooking lived up to their promise. After dessert we all crowded into the parlor. The adults started talking about different things. We children began to feel bored, and just a bit restless.

"Can we go out to the barn?" Barney asked no one in particular after checking to see if the other kids wanted to go.

"I suppose it would be all right. What do you think?" Dad asked the other adults.

"Sure . . . but dress warmly," was Mom's reply.

When we got outside, we could see a sky filled with stars. They shone brightly enough on the snow so that we could easily see our way to the barn.

"Let's play hide-and-seek," said Nell, as we started to run to the barn. "Okay!" we all agreed, as we rushed in.

But when we were in the barn, we noticed that the lights were not very bright. The place looked scary. We stayed together, and carefully explored. We visited Boxer and Bonnie. They were surprised to see seven children wanting to rub their sides and noses and feed them hay. But they didn't seem to mind at all.

Then we went to Elsie's stall. She mooed and acted out of sorts as we crowded around her. We decided she wanted to be left alone.

"Look at all this stuff," Kathleen said,

pointing to the area where Grandpa stored his bridles and harnesses and other things. As each piece was picked up and explored, we tried to give a name to each one.

Off to the side, all on its own, was a harness that didn't look like any of the other pieces. It seemed to be really, really old. And it was smaller than all the others. "What's this for?" Nell asked, carefully lifting it up.

"It's gotta be a harness," Barney replied, sounding as if he had spent his whole life on a farm.

"But it looks different," I said, as Nell passed it to me. "It looks as if it's for a small horse or donkey."

The more I looked at the harness and held it, the stranger it appeared to be. It almost had a glow to it, although it was dark brown in color.

"Hey! Over here!" Em and Will shouted. "Look at this." They stood before a door that none of us had ever noticed before. The door had opened, revealing a long set of

stairs leading down. It was hard to see what was at the bottom, but a sparkling white light was shining.

"Let's go," said Barney, putting his foot on the first step. "Yeah, let's see what's down there," added Nell.

"I don't know," cautioned Will, "maybe we should check with Grandpa." "Yeah, let's explore it during the daytime," suggested Kathleen.

"It's only a set of steps in an old barn," Nell said confidently. "I'm going to have a look."

With Nell leading, we all headed down the stairs behind a door that we had never seen before. Nothing that anyone could have told us would have prepared us for what happened next.

WHEN we got to the bottom, we found ourselves outside again. We should have been below ground but here we were in a place that we did not recognize.

"I'm going back," said Will. "I've had enough strange things happen to me for one day."

But when he turned around to go back up the stairs, they were not there any more.

"What's going on?" wondered Em, with a hint of fear in her voice.

"I'm scared," said Tim, who grabbed my hand. I noticed I was still holding the small harness, which now was the only sign that just seconds ago we had been in Grandpa's barn.

We formed a little circle together and slowly looked around. The night was not as cold as when we had run to the barn. It was chilly, but there was no snow anywhere, and there was grass on the ground. We were in a field surrounded on three sides by hills. The fourth side sloped down to what looked to be a tiny village. We could see the outline of small buildings, and lights were shining in some of them.

Above us the sky was full of stars. We could even see shooting stars. But what caught our attention was an unusually bright star, shining high above the little village. It gave out the sparkling white light that had attracted us when we noticed the open door in the barn.

"What happened to those stairs?" Barney asked. "Let's find them and get out of here." We agreed to split into two groups and to look around us for a way out. But there was nothing to be found in the field.

"The only thing to do is to find someone who can help us," suggested Tim.

"Yeah, let's walk down to the village," said his sister Nell.

"I'm tired," complained Will. "I can't walk all the way."

"You have to try," Barney said. "If we don't get back, we'll miss Christmas Eve, and we'll be in trouble."

We agreed that we'd help Will if he couldn't make it all the way. Then we started walking toward the village.

"Hey, that's the Big Dipper over there," I said. "That means we're walking toward the east. Dad says that long ago they used to call the Big Dipper the Big Bear. But it looks more like a dipper to me."

I had hoped to distract everyone so they wouldn't be so afraid. We were all a little scared and confused.

"Look, Will," I said, "there beside the North Star is a great big 'W'—the first letter of your name." Dad had always liked to point out the stars to Will when we watched the sky in the summer. "There are your stars, Will," he'd say as he pointed to the northeast sky.

The sky was unusually bright. It seemed as if the sparkling white star over the village was leading us on. We had no trouble finding our way through the night because of its glow. Still, we did not see anyone else.

The star seemed to shine on a few buildings just outside the town. Without thinking or discussing what we were doing, we were drawn to the place where the star pointed.

"Is everyone okay?" I asked.

"I don't know," answered Kathleen, weakly.

"I'm okay," said Em. "You know, there must be a reason why we're here, why this is happening to us."

"What makes you so sure?" Tim questioned Em.

"I can't really say . . . it's just a feeling," Em replied.

As we got nearer the village, it was clear

that the light was leading to a single building,
set away from the rest.

"I think it's a barn," Barney said.

"Yeah, well, it sure doesn't look like
Grandpa's barn," added Nell.

"I know that," said Barney. "But, look,
there are animals inside, and there are people
in there, too!"

We could all see the building clearly now.

There was a big door half open, and a light, not bright, but like that from an oil lamp, in the barn.

As we approached, we could feel a warm and safe sense about the barn. We went forward slowly. Not one of us said anything. We went in softly and quietly. The animals were still and calm in their stalls. Then we saw where the people were. First, we saw some men and boys with shepherds' staffs. Then there were girls and women in white gowns. Finally, we saw a man standing, and beside him, resting in the straw, was a woman who was lifting up a tiny, newborn child.

The baby was not all quiet and sleepy, as I used to imagine. This was a real baby, crying and upset. I watched the woman lift the baby from a straw bed that was covered with cloth and hold it close to her. Everyone else, all the creatures, all the people, became very still. The baby soon became quiet, content in the care of its mother.

There was a wonderful look on the faces

of the man and the woman. The baby, as it took comfort from the woman, had the same wonderful look. The glow on their faces reached out to each one of us who stood watching the mystery of the barn, with all its animals and visitors gathered around the newborn baby and its parents.

After the baby had been fed, the mother gently offered the child to the man, who held him close and laid him down in the little bed that was prepared for the baby. The baby looked out at each one of us through warm, contented eyes that gradually closed in peaceful sleep.

In the quiet of the place, each one of us seemed to become aware of the gentle in-and-out of our own breathing. The man and the woman looked at one another with the deepest look of caring. Then they looked toward those of us who had gathered, and they shared that look with us. Their look filled us and held us close together in the most tender way.

After a time—I can't say how long—the man noticed the harness I was still carrying in my right hand, the one that we had found in Grandpa's barn. He walked over to me, and I offered him the harness. He smiled and walked over to the donkey that was standing near the baby. He patted the donkey's flank and hung the harness on the wall.

All was well in the barn. We seven who had come through the door and down the stairs in our grandparents' barn on Christmas Eve looked at one another and back at the woman, the man, and the baby. With happy smiles on our faces, we turned to go. We noticed that a door in the barn was open, waiting for us, a door like the one in Grandpa's barn. There were stairs leading up. We each glanced back at the baby and its parents as we turned to leave. At the top of the stairs, a door opened into Grandpa's barn.

We headed back to the house. The sky was still full of stars, but not the bright one that had led us to Christmas.

"I guess you were right, Em," Nell said. "There was a reason for us being here tonight. We made a real journey to Christmas."

As we took off our coats and boots, we heard the adults singing a Christmas carol: *"Away in a manger, no crib for his bed, the little Lord Jesus laid down his sweet head. . . ."*

"What's a manger?" Will asked, as we joined them around Grandma's piano. "Is it a barn?"

"Yes, it is the place in the barn where the animals feed, where the hay is put out for them," Mom said.

"That's what I thought," said Will, reflectively.

We sang another carol.

"Silent night, holy night, all is calm, all is bright. Round yon virgin mother and child. . . ."

THE next morning, after we had given out our gifts, I went back out to the barn. Although I had given the harness to the baby's father the night before, it was back in place where we had found it. Every Christmas we spent on the farm I would look for it, and it would always be there in its special place.

Just before Grandpa died, when I was in my final year at college, and we had our last Christmas at the farm, Grandpa took me aside and he gave me the harness to keep. "But it's not just for you, you know. I want you to have it because you know how important it is."

I didn't know what to say. I wasn't sure if I was the one to have it.

"I want you to," he insisted. "You know, it's taken me a long time to realize that the most important things we have to give to one another can't be bought. Here," he said, handing it over to me, "take care of it for the family."

"It seems to me," he added, "barns become holy places at Christmas time. Keep this in a special place where children and even older folks can discover it."

I'VE tried to take care of the donkey's harness that Grandpa handed on to us. When I was able to, I bought a place in the country. It isn't a real working farm like the one Grandpa and Grandma had. But it has a barn. I keep the harness there.

Our family gathers at our place for Christmas. And on certain Christmas eves, my children, and now my grandchildren, go out to the barn after dinner.

We older folks stay by the fire and remember the time that Grandpa came to get us at the train station in his sleigh and Boxer and Bonnie took us home safely through the snowstorm. We talk about how Em saved

Will from the snow plow, and we recall our mysterious Christmas journey. Each time, I feel close to Em and Will and Barney and Kathleen and Tim and Nell in the same special way that I experienced that strange night long ago.

We're singing our favorite Christmas carols when the children come back in. They look so amazed and yet are so very quiet. Our eyes meet theirs, as they gather around to join us in our singing. The glow on their faces and in their eyes tells us that they have begun their own mysterious journey to Christmas.